FAIR PLAY

~ Poems for William Shakespeare
on the occasion of his CDLVIIth Birthday
from XII Meeter Ballad-Mongers ~

SDPF

Fair Play
Edited by Janice Dempsey

First Edition

Mary Baker Muir, Dónall Dempsey, Richard Williams, Laura
Theis, John Wheeler, Jenna Plewes, Simon Williams, Georgia
Hilton, Jeremy Loynes, Claudia Court, Timothy Adès and Barry
Smith have asserted their authorship and given their permission to
Dempsey & Windle for these poems to be published here.

Published by Dempsey & Windle
15 Rosetrees
Guildford
Surrey
GU1 2HS
UK
01483 571164
dempseyandwindle.com

British Library Cataloguing-in-Publication Data

A catalogue record for this book is available from the British
Library

ISBN: 978-1-913329-53-2

Printed and bound in the UK

CONTENTS

Welcome to the South Downs Poetry Festival and Dempsey & Windle Publishing's celebration of William Shakespeare, on the occasion of the four hundred and fifty-seventh anniversary of his probable birth and the four hundred and fifth anniversary of his death. In this period of pandemic we got together online to share the poems of the Bard of Avon, and also invited eleven of our recently published poets to read poems they have written in response his timeless work. We were joined by Barry Smith, the director of the Festival, (himself a widely published poet) and two accomplished actors, Paula Tinker reading from *The Merchant of Venice* and Gareth Williams reading from *As You Like It.*

I say 'probable birth' because everything about William Shakespeare's life and work — including his very identity as the author of his plays — has been questioned over the past four hundred years. With at least seventeen different spellings of his name used by Will himself, and scant public records of his transactions in Elizabethan and Jacobean society, it's taken scholarship (of varying quality and in many instances a lot of imagination) to construct a tentative biography of the actor and writer whose work we call 'Shakespearean'.

Almost forgotten for two hundred years after his death, Shakespeare's plays were only preserved by his friends and colleagues, John Hemings and Henry Condell, who transcribed and published them in a badly printed book now known as 'The First Folio', in 1623, some seven years after Shakespeare's death. Interest in the plays revived in the nineteenth century and the question of Shakespeare's identity attracted several cranks and eccentrics, as well as respectable scholars, to propound various theories of 'who wrote Shakespeare.' Francis Bacon and the Earl of Southampton are two candidates, both largely debunked by modern scholars.

As well as the plays, (many at least partly written in collaboration with other actors) Shakespeare was the author of poems. A long poem titled 'Venus and Adonis' survives. The best known of his poems are the 154 sonnets, most of them addressed to the Earl of Southampton, with a section dedicated to the so-called 'Dark Lady'. Like so much else in Shakespeare's life, there's a mystery surrounding the identity, the true gender, and indeed the existence outside the poet's own imagination, of the Dark Lady.

Scattered, rewritten, stolen, defaced, brutally edited and bowdlerised, or simply mislaid, copies and fragments of the First Folio have been painstakingly collected and housed in the Folger Shakespeare Library in Washington DC. The library now houses thousands of primary documents, and copies of treatises, critics' works and biographies connected with Shakespeare. Research and the impact on the English language of Shakespeare's vivid metaphorical inventions and neologisms continue unabated into our own century.

We assert that the Bard of Avon was indeed the author of those wise, humane plays and lyrical poems, whose rich, imaginative use of the English language enables his words to transcend their historical context and speak to us of humanity's universal concerns of birth, life, love and death.

Our title, *Fair Play*, is one of the multitude of phrases and metaphors that Shakespeare has bequeathed to the English language, so familiar that we take them for granted and use them without thinking, four hundred and five years after the death of the literary genius that was William Shakespeare. And in the subtitle, 'Meeter Ballad-Mongers' was his colourful term for the writers of poems.

Janice Dempsey
Editor

Being and Nothingness

(Lines on sorting a book collection)

To be or not to be, that is the question
which has bedevilled our existential angst
since William Shakespeare – or was it Thomas Kyd? –
crystallised our dizzying predicament.
And so, Jean Paul, here's the rub, for I weigh
your fate, like a bare bodkin, in my hand
poised betwixt the suffocating dark
or temporary reprieve to rest
amongst the riddling heroes of the pen,
to hold, as 'twere, the mirror up to man.

Alas, poor Sartre, liberated one day
from sedately curated shelves of academe
between black coffee in the campus bar
and metaphysical poetry seminar,
left-bank arbiter of hawks and handsaws,
embodies for a while that cool ennui,
somnambulantly drifts through long neglect,
to sleep, perchance to dream, in dusty
seclusion, king of shreds and patches
bounded in a nutshell of infinite space.

By indirections we find directions out:
your magnum opus, fretful high-wire act
awaits the determinant curtain call,
but the rest, as the man said, is silence.

Barry Smith

First published in Acumen, vol.87, Jan 2017

Sonnet No. XXXIII

Full many a glorious morning have I seen
Flatter the mountain tops with sovereign eye,
Kissing with golden face the meadows green,
Gilding pale streams with heavenly alchemy;

Anon permit the basest clouds to ride
With ugly rack on his celestial face,
And from the forlorn world his visage hide,
Stealing unseen to west with this disgrace:

Even so my sun one early morn did shine,
With all triumphant splendour on my brow;
But out, alack, he was but one hour mine,
The region cloud hath mask'd him from me now

Yet him for this my love no whit disdaineth;
Suns of the world may stain when heaven's sun staineth.

William Shakespeare

Return

House martins are back
to dance their blistering jigsaw
through the sycamores' familiar sky

Kiss kiss kiss
house martins whisper me
forage tucked behind the hopper

flick and flicker
blasting autonomous
to message summer over an eggwhite sky

Happiness comes fast and monotone
an orchestra of black-tipped streaks
spinning below the sacrificial Sussex down
whisper another fledgling future.

Mary Baker Muir

9

My Love is as a Fever...Longing Still

All that long hot summer through
I shared a summer cold with you

that seemed to last forever. Whether

sharing the same germs, dreams,
bacteria or whatever

it seemed to bind us so...very close together.

If this was love...it couldn't get no better.

And all my heart could say
even to this day...is:

'Bless you...bless you...bless you.'

Friends of mine who had been childhood sweethearts were coming up to their golden wedding anniversary. They had everything...the big house...well-off etc. They were telling me when they first got together they had a flat with not a stick of furniture and slept on bare floorboards. They had nothing except each other and an illustrated Shakespeare's Sonnets. I told them I would write a poem for them. But he died only days before the big day and she only a few days later. So it was at their funeral that I ended up blessing their love.

Dónall Dempsey

Sister Hamlet

Oh, I still remember
your Hamlet
(the best production I ever saw)

you home from school
wrapping yourself in the crimson curtain
of our living room

& stabbing yourself
in the arras
& crying: " a rat...a rat! "

& how something or other was rotten
& bringing the curtain down
upon your dying

annoying our mother
critical of your over-heated performance
she sending us (like a bad review) scampering

I will remember
your Shakespeare
to my dying day

your eyes wild
your hair flying
and how

with an entire
cast of you
you acted it out

to my open and gasping
mouth drinking you in
with my thirsty mind

Shakespeare come
startlingly alive me peppered
with beauty & spittle

oh, sister Hamlet
I still live in the wonder
of your telling

'If you tickle us...'

The moon intently listens
to the open air

production of
The Merchant of Venice

— in Venice —

this delicious summer's night
(hemmed in by houses)

where we discover that

The quality of mercy
is not
strained...

as a couple upstairs
come home and proceed to make
long loud passionate love

...it droppeth like...
another couple scream and fight
as windows smash and plates crash

...the gentle rain from Heaven...

'Agghhh! '
'Cazzo in culo!'

and throws his clothes out
the now broken window

...upon the earth below...

as a gondola ghosts by in mist
with an atrocious tourist version of
'O Sole Mio! '

as another window lights up
and a telly bellows
a dubbed gangster shoot-out.

'Aggggh!'
'Va fancip!'

We are enthralled with
(delighted and enraptured)

not only with
the splendour that is Shakespeare

but also with the real-life drama

of this gentle Italian night
and of how we got

our *pound of flesh.*

* * *

On first looking into Mr. Shakespeare

I step out of the here & now
slip into the space between
second (&) second.
Time scowls: 'Oh...don't tell me
I've lost...him again!'

Invisible to all
in my window seat

I again that little boy

letting the world go by
(hidden in a heartbeat)

lost in *The Tempest*
of words

caught between the thresholds
of worlds upon worlds.

'Come to me...
...with a thought!'
the big black book calls

'Your thoughts...
...I cleave to!'
I whisper to its words.

I all at once my own
Prospero & Ariel

set free from the knotted
pine of dyslexia

thanks to Mr. Shakespeare's
spell.

Dónall Dempsey

14

Shakespeare and Football

My father is a huge Shakespeare fan. To the extent that for many family birthdays, from I think the age of about 8, we would go on a surprise trip where we always seemed to end up in Stratford.

I wrote a senru about one of these trips; it has a title...

On Being Taken To Watch Akira Kurosawa's Japanese Version of Macbeth for My Twelfth Birthday when all I Wanted to Do was Go to the Football

> deceit and hubris
> leads to lengthening speeches
> everybody dies.

I did learn to enjoy Shakespeare, partly through Kurosawa's films and other trips to the RSC and elsewhere.

Shakespeare probably played football when he was young, and mentions it in a couple of plays. in the Comedy of Errors Dromio says;

Am I so round with you as you with me
That like a football you do spurn me thus?
You spurn me hence, and he will spurn me hither.
If I last in this service, you must case me in leather.

Football in Shakespeare's time was very different to how it is now. In a seventeenth century book Philip Stubbes describes it as a 'friendly kind of fight'...sometimes their necks are broken, sometimes their backs, sometimes their legs, sometimes their arms, sometime one part thrust out of joint, sometime another, sometime their noses gush out with blood, sometimes their eyes start out.

Apparently, more people died playing football than died through sword fights or archery. No wonder it was banned.

Richard Williams

Sonnet No. L

How heavy do I journey on the way,
When what I seek, my weary travel's end,
Doth teach that ease and that repose to say,
"Thus far the miles are measur'd from thy friend!"
The beast that bears me, tired with my woe,
Plods dully on, to bear that weight in me,
As if by some instinct the wretch did know
His rider lov'd not speed, being made from thee:
The bloody spur cannot provoke him on
That sometimes anger thrusts into his hide;
Which heavily he answers with a groan,
More sharp to me than spurring to his side;
    For that same groan doth put this in my mind;
    My grief lies onward, and my joy behind.

William Shakespeare

reading shakespeare by the lakeside

I am alone today
that is
I'm not really alone

what I mean is
I've got the lake
to myself

sharing only with a handful
of dark-feathered ducks
that look like

preachers
with their white collars
their stretched-out wings

and I've got a dog-eared copy of the tempest
so in a way I've got him too: Bill

as I call him affectionately
that marvellous dream-weaver whose legacy
is enshrined
in our language

between him and the
chattering ducks I have all
the company I need

Laura Theis

Three Shakespeare Blackouts

Blackout: HAMLET

TO BE A SEA
TO SLEEP MORE
TO SAY THAT IN THAT SLEEP
DREAMS MAY COIL

LIFE MUST PAUSE
FOR SO LONG THAT
NO TRAVELLER
WILL FLY TO OTHER COWARDS
OR REGARD THEIR CURRENT NAME

Blackout: ROMEO AND JULIET

SOFT LIGHT IS ENVIOUS
THE MOON ALREADY PALE

IT IS MY ANSWER:
I AM THE FAIREST

I RETURN THE BRIGHTNESS TO
SHAME THOSE STARS

HER EYES WERE NOT THE NIGHT
O THAT I WERE

Blackout: MIDSUMMER NIGHT'S DREAM

I AM LIKE
UNEARNED LUCK:
THE SERPENT
A LIAR

GIVE ME
YOUR FRIENDS'
GENTLE WONDER
BUT MAKE ALL THINGS PLAIN

YOU WOULD KNOW THIS BEAUTY AND
THIS MAN:
ROUGH, VILE, GRISLY
COMING FIRST BY NIGHT...

AS SHE FLED BLOODY I GREW BRAVE:
FOUND HIS BLADE
(ALL THE REST REMAIN
AT LARGE)

Laura Theis

(Blackout poems are constructed by cutting and pasting lines from another writer's work.)

Allegro / fine (*An automotive soliloquy*)

My Allegro! First and only car
in Reynard gold whose flecks outshone the sun.
A joy! A bulwark 'gainst the wayward bus
uncertain train and all the vagaries
of weather sent to sweep a London street.

A pride it was, mine own though small enough.
It sent me trav'ling thoughtless roads apace.
A prince of men - this Austin was all mine!

And so I drove unheeding of my fate
Not knowing then that mis'ry could be great.

For there! The white van man did sally forth
with tee shirt short and half a can of coke.

Oft-times do I descry his brethren horde
upon the Walworth Road or Southwark Bridge.
But now came he with passing fury out
from some small side road hid between the trees
and ripped my car untimely from the road.

In shock and dread I clambered from the wreck.
Oh wounded, sadly twisted was my car!
While his white beast had suffered but a scratch.

I stroked and stilled the quiet roof with love.

Rough-voiced recov'ry men did force and drag
the shattered frame upon their greasy truck.
And it was gone. No more to be my pride.

And then, to insult further, rubbing bitter
salt into a gaping new-made wound,
the man from Norwich Union did then
decide to offer me but fifty pounds...

Long gone now, my ancient noble car.
But sometimes I do look above to see,
Allegro there — in all its majesty!

John Wheeler

Writing on water

Ink loses its solidity and line
and with each touch the pattern is less certain.
Ripples and reflections mix the words
so over time it's harder to recall
the slip and flow of things that went before
to beach us at this place.

Each soft daily drip of moment wears
the crisp hard angles, edged extremities,
and those we knew in sharp relief in all
their angers, tide-swept struggling, and embittered
tears, become as thin as crystal dewdrops
on summer evening grass.

'Good father. Yes he was. And she was kind.
 I always heard it so. The stories that
they told! But then, I don't remember them
the way I did... And they were really good
at...something once. Yes, I must look it up...'
 But then I never do.

Instead, unshaped in old grey coat and hood
I chant goodbyes and pull the front door wide –
then write my way with footsteps on a street
And sometimes turn
to watch them all
dissolve into the rain.

John Wheeler

The Naming of Moons

Your moonstruck lives spin threads
in space, circle the Greek God of the sky.
Your voices drifting through the galaxies;
a stardust skein of memories.

Titania, Oberon, fleet-footed Puck,
Ariel, Cordelia, long lost Perdita,
Miranda, Prospero, misshapen Caliban,
love-broken Desdemona, Juliet, Ophelia -

We cannot meet you on your moons, or
see your first step off the page; and yet
we know ourselves in you, walk in your shoes.

We've been in love, and out of love and been deceived,
we've known despair, gone to the edge, pulled back. Yet
you scale peaks, plumb depths we only tiptoe past.

Uranus has 27 known moons, 25 of them named after
Shakespeare's characters.

Jenna Plewes

The Second-Best Bed Speaks

I was their privacy, their playground,
a small, close-curtained world
of sighs, soft words and foolishness.

Rustle of nightclothes sliding to the floor,
tangle and tumble of limb with limb,
skin against skin, lip on lip.

Place your fingers on my carved oak frame,
stroke the mirror-polish of my secrecy,
listen to my centuries of silence.

Feel yielding featherbed and wool;
loving was here, bedding, birthing and dying,
I held their joys and sorrows, knew them best.

Shakespeare left the second-best bed to Anne in his will.

Jenna Plewes

Sonnet No. CXVI

Let me not to the marriage of true minds
Admit impediments.
Love is not love
Which alters when it alteration finds,
Or bends with the remover to remove:
O no! it is an ever-fixed mark
That looks on tempests and is never shaken;
It is the star to every wandering bark,
Whose worth's unknown, although his height be taken.
Love's not Time's fool, though rosy lips and cheeks
Within his bending sickle's compass come:
Love alters not with his brief hours and weeks,
But bears it out even to the edge of doom.
    If this be error and upon me proved,
    I never writ, nor no man ever loved.

William Shakespeare

Shakespeare In Love

Let's start with young Will Shakespeare, jobbing hack,
who sells the same play twice, with no word written.
Romance is what he wants, an inside track
to how and why his heroine is smitten.

Then there's Viola, early theatre fan,
so wants to cheer on stage, not from the stalls,
can't get around the Revel Master's ban,
auditions anyway, which takes some balls.

Our Will's no dolt, can tell a woman's shape,
asks her to stay for 'special study sessions'
and once in bed, his storyline reshapes
to make a passion from an indiscretion,

so never was a play more brilliant
than this Viola and her William.

Simon Williams

Shakespearean Banquet

'Have you seen the menu? What sonnet?'
                                    Marc Woodward

To start
Hamlet; a very small slice of ham
with a garnish of mustard and cressida.
The flaming of the stew of lamb
(from the cookbook of Burger King Lear).

Main courses
A midsummer night's bream
with a Julius Caesar salad.
A sauce of shylocks in cream,
on a merchant of venison roulade.
Much ragout about mutton,
with more than a pound of meat.
Cow pie for Falstaffian gluttons
and bubble, bubble, toil and squeak.

Desserts
Have what you like, as you like it.
All's well that ends well at a banquet.

                                    Simon Williams

Lockdown Easing in Verona

Two households – if both alike in dignity can
now meet up outside.

Don't forget – civil
hands must be clean before & after mutiny.

Georgia Hilton

Counting beans

A soliloquy in the style of Shakespeare

Hah! What's in a life that's worth a bean?
And we that live it
What makes us more than mere machines
Going through the motions?

It's the inner life that makes us real
What we know and think and feel
The journey of the spirit like a shining wheel
Rolling out the true measure of our days.

What's in a life that's really worth a bean?
Not the daily grind, the mind-numbing routine
Not the waste, the ugliness that makes you want to scream
Of people trapped in lives they simply do not mean.

This dubious collection of flesh and bones is just a frail frame
A flimsy lampshade hung about the inner flame
When we are lost and broken, shipwrecked, shattered
The enduring fire within is all, and all that matters.

Jeremy Loynes

First published in 'Turning' by Jeremy Loynes (Dempsey & Windle 2017)

How?

A tribute to William Shakespeare

How, Will?
Oh how was it you knew us all
so well?
You, the country boy,
the glove-maker's son from nowhere —
backwater Bill from sleepy Stratford.
Wasn't that what they first thought of you —
those other writers?
Before the ink was dry
they weren't scoffing any longer.

And was it there, in not-so sleepy Stratford,
in your father's workshop, making gloves,
that, finger by finger,
you first learned to turn us inside out —
to reveal our inner fabric?
Our hopes, despairs — our jealousies and secret dreams,
rough, misshapen,
flawed, mistaken,
coming apart at the seams.

Where did you find the mirror, Will?
The perfect glass
to show as we are,
troubled and tormented,
yet still wondering at the stars.

How was it you knew us all
so well?
Every man and every woman,

every struggling soul and spirit,
what it means to be here – to be human.
Oh, the star-crossed lovers!
Oh, the power-mad and ruthless kings!
How was it that you knew us all?
That you knew everything?

How is it what you showed us
still touches us today?
It seems we've moved on, we've changed,
in this sophisticated age.
But, truth be told,
you're still with us –
your text still burns upon the page
And we're still captive –
still listening, amazed,
we're still pictured in your gaze,
we're still standing on your stage.

Jeremy Loynes

Sonnet No. LXI

Is it thy will thy image should keep open
My heavy eyelids to the weary night?
Dost thou desire my slumbers should be broken,
While shadows like to thee do mock my sight?
Is it thy spirit that thou send'st from thee
So far from home into my deeds to pry,
To find out shames and idle hours in me,
The scope and tenor of thy jealousy?
O, no! thy love, though much, is not so great:
It is my love that keeps mine eye awake;
Mine own true love that doth my rest defeat,
To play the watchman ever for thy sake:
    For thee watch I whilst thou dost wake elsewhere,
    From me far off, with others all too near.

William Shakespeare

When the Time Comes

The heat turns your cheek
pink, lights the dark as flame
spits from dampened logs
in the rough-edged grate

hissing above sighs of wind
that lean down the chimney
yearning for shelter
from the pitch of night.

You raise a glass – deep
damson-red liquid
quivering with baubles
of firelight. You drink

to the life you've lived
the adventures shared.
And you close your eyes
till you've disappeared.

Claudia Court

JOHN OF GAUNT — from 'Richard the Second'

This royal throne of kings, this sceptred isle,
This earth of majesty, this seat of Mars,
This other Eden, demi-paradise,
This fortress built by Nature for herself
Against infection and the hand of war,
This happy breed of men, this little world,
This precious stone set in the silver sea
Which serves it in the office of a wall
Or as a moat defensive to a house,
Against the envy of less happier lands,
This blessed plot, this earth, this realm, this England,
This nurse, this teeming womb of royal kings,
Feared by their breed and famous for their birth,
Renownèd for their deeds as far from home
For Christian service and true chivalry
As is the sepulchre in stubborn Jewry
Of the world's ransom, blessèd Mary's son.
This land of such dear souls, this dear, dear land,
Dear for her reputation through the world,
Is now leased out - I die pronouncing it -
Like to a tenement or pelting farm.
England, bound in with the triumphant sea,
Whose rocky shore beats back the envious siege
Of watery Neptune, is now bound in with shame,
With inky blots and rotten parchment bonds.
That England that was wont to conquer others
Hath made a shameful conquest of itself.
Ah, would the scandal vanish with my life,
How happy then were my ensuing death!

William Shakespeare
Richard II Act 2 Sc 3

Sonnet No. 107: Your Immortality in my Words

Timothy has rewritten all Shakespeare's sonnets as lipograms, that is, he has avoided using one or more letters. The letter not used is E.

Not my misgivings, nor this vast world's soul,
clairvoyant, musing on futurity,
can bring my loving-span within control,
in pawn to prison of mortality.
Now mortal moon has known its black occlusion,
sad augurs mock old words of doom miscast,
doubts put on crowns, abjuring all confusion,
orchards flaunt fruits pacific. Conflict's past.
My darling's blooming in this balmy day!
What of old Dis? I'm not afraid of him:
I'll last by my poor rhyming, anyway,
whilst Dis shall bully folk too dumb, too dim;

and this your tumulus shall long surpass
vain tyrants' coats-of-arms and tombs of brass.

Dis, or Pluto: grim god of Tartarus

Timothy Adès

First published in 'Loving by Will' by Timothy Adès (Dempsey & Windle, 2017) which contains all 154 sonnets, with lipograms of each of them.

The Poets

Timothy Adès is a rhyming translator-poet with several books, mostly bilingual, from French and Spanish, and awards for translating Victor Hugo, Robert Desnos, Jean Cassou, and Alfonso Reyes. Other favourites are Brecht, Sikelianós, and Ricarda Huch. He is on www.brindinpress.com, www.timothyades.com, and YouTube.

Claudia Court has had work published in a number of magazines and anthologies, and won several competitions. Her debut collection, *How to Punctuate a Silence*, was published during lockdown in 2020 by Dempsey and Windle.

Dónall Dempsey, originally from Ireland, has four collections of poetry and is co-owner/editor of Dempsey & Windle Publishing. In non-pandemic times he comperes 'The 1000 Monkeys' monthly open mic night. His poems have been published extensively, in UK and internationally, in anthologies and journals, printed and online.

Georgia Hilton is an Irish poet and fiction writer living in Winchester, England. Her poem 'Dark-Haired Hilda Replies to Patrick Kavanagh' won the Brian Dempsey Memorial Prize in 2018, and she has a pamphlet *I went up the lane quite cheerful* and a collection *Swing,* both published by Dempsey and Windle. Her short fiction has appeared in *Lunate Fiction, Fictive Dream* and the Didcot Writers anthology. Georgia tweets sometimes at @GGeorgiahilton.

Jeremy Loynes has always enjoyed creative writing and likes the challenge of trying to capture a thought, image or idea in a few lines. The natural world and the voices of Edward Thomas and Robert Frost are often in his thoughts. His first collection, *Turning,* was published in 2017 by Dempsey & Windle.

Mary Baker Muir is an Edinburgh Scot now living in London. Former editor of the St. Andrews literary magazine, teacher and business consultant, who on retiring from full-time work was able to start sending out work to publishers. Many have now been published in print and online and her first poetry collection EX SITU came out from Dempsey & Windle in summer 2020.

Jenna Plewes's poetry is in anthologies and magazines. She has published six collections: *The Salt and Sweet of Memory,* (Dempsey & Windle, 2019) and *The Underside of Things* (winner of the Hedgehog Poetry Press Competition 2020) raised £1250 for charity; *A Woven Rope* (V. Press 2021) is also being sold for charity.

Barry Smith is co-ordinator of the Festival of Chichester and director of the South Downs Poetry Festival. Widely published in anthologies and magazines, he was runner-up in the BBC Proms Poetry competition. Barry is editor of *Poetry & All That Jazz,* curates the poetry for Blakefest and works as a performance poet.

Laura Theis' debut collection *how to extricate yourself* was the winner of the 2020 Brian Dempsey Memorial Pamphlet Prize. Her work has been internationally published in numerous anthologies and literary journals. She has won an A.M. Heath Prize, the Hammond House International Literary Award and the Mogford Short Story Prize. lauratheis.weebly.com.

John Wheeler is a performance poet and multiple poetry-slam winner. His work has also been short-listed for the Bridport

International Poetry Competition and selected for a range of anthologies. His collection *What did I just say?* was published in 2018.

Richard Williams lives in Portsmouth and has had poems in a range of print and online magazines, including *Acumen, Envoi, Frogmore Papers, One Hand Clapping* and *Orbis.* Others have appeared on radio, including the BBC. A first collection, *Landings*, was published by Dempsey & Windle in 2018.

Simon Williams has been writing since his teens, when he was mentored at university by Roger McGough. He has nine collections; the latest is *The Magpie Almanack* (VOLE, 2020) available at www.simonwilliams.info. Simon was elected The Bard of Exeter in 2013, founded the large-format magazine, The Broadsheet, and published the PLAY anthology in 2018.